The Bank Account Mirror

The Bank Account Mirror

Matthew Petchinsky

1

The Bank Account Mirror: Healing How You See Yourself Through Money

By: Matthew Petchinsky

Disclaimer

This book, *The Bank Account Mirror: Healing How You See Yourself Through Money*, is an exploratory and reflective work focused on identity formation, emotional awareness, and personal perception as they relate to money. It is designed to help readers examine the symbolic, psychological, and experiential relationship they have with finances—not to instruct, direct, or advise on financial decision-making.

Nothing in this book constitutes financial, legal, accounting, investment, tax, or professional advice of any kind. The content is not intended to replace guidance from qualified professionals such as financial advisors, accountants, attorneys, therapists, or counselors. Any financial concepts discussed are presented solely as metaphors, reflections, or illustrative examples meant to support self-inquiry and emotional understanding.

All exercises, reflections, journaling prompts, and perspectives offered in this book are voluntary and intended for personal growth purposes only. Readers are solely responsible for how they interpret and apply the material. Financial outcomes, emotional shifts, or personal insights will vary from person to person, and no guarantees—explicit or implied—are made regarding results, income, stability, or personal transformation.

This book does not diagnose, treat, cure, or prevent any mental health condition. If engaging with themes of money, self-worth, scarcity, or identity brings up emotional distress, anxiety, or discomfort, readers are encouraged to pause and seek support from a licensed mental health professional.

By reading this book, you acknowledge that you are engaging with reflective material for educational and self-development purposes only and that all financial and life decisions remain entirely your own responsibility.

This work is intended as a mirror—not a map—inviting awareness, not instruction; insight, not advice.

Introduction

Your balance doesn't define your being.

Yet for most people, it quietly does.

Not in obvious ways. Not in statements spoken out loud. But in the way the chest tightens before opening a banking app. In the way confidence rises or collapses based on a number that changes without warning. In the way self-respect, safety, and even worth are silently negotiated through dollar signs.

Money has become a mirror—one so polished and ever-present that many no longer recognize it as a reflection at all. They mistake it for truth.

This book exists to interrupt that illusion.

The Bank Account Mirror is not about earning more, spending better, or mastering financial systems. It is about understanding how deeply money has been allowed to define identity—and how quietly that definition shapes decisions, self-talk, relationships, ambition, shame, and hope. For many, money is no longer a tool; it is a verdict. A scorecard. A measure of who they believe they are allowed to be.

But a mirror only shows what stands before it. It does not create the person looking back.

What if your bank account was never the problem—but simply a surface reflecting unresolved beliefs, inherited narratives, emotional conditioning, and survival responses? What if the numbers you see are not proof of failure or success, but echoes of stories learned long before you had the language to question them?

This guide is an invitation to dismantle that mirror.

Not by smashing it in anger, and not by replacing it with affirmations or fantasies—but by stepping back far enough to see it clearly. To recognize when money has been mistaken for identity, when scarcity has been internalized as character, and when abundance has been confused with worthiness.

Within these pages, you will be guided to separate *who you are* from *what you have*, and to reconnect with a deeper, steadier sense of self that exists before numbers, beyond balances, and independent of financial fluctuation. This is not about denying reality or ignoring responsibility. It is about reclaiming authorship over the meaning you assign to money—and releasing the meanings that were never yours to carry.

When identity is fused to income, peace becomes conditional. Confidence becomes fragile. And self-trust erodes every time the numbers change. This book offers another way: a grounded, honest reconnection to truth—one where money is placed back into its proper role, and you are restored to yours.

You are not your balance.

You never were.

This book helps you remember that—and shows you how to live from that truth.

Chapter 1: Money as a Mirror of the Self

Money Reflects, It Does Not Define

Money does not arrive in your life as a judgment, yet it is often experienced as one. From early on, numbers become symbols—of safety, approval, intelligence, success, or failure—long before they represent actual purchasing power. A low balance can trigger shame, while a higher one can momentarily inflate confidence, even though neither changes the essence of who you are. This emotional reaction reveals that money is functioning as a mirror, reflecting internal beliefs rather than external truth.

When money feels personal, it is because it has been fused with identity. The mind interprets financial circumstances as evidence of character, discipline, or worthiness, despite money being influenced by systems, timing, health, access, and inherited conditions. The reflection becomes distorted when circumstances are mistaken for self-definition. Understanding this separation is the first step toward reclaiming agency over how you see yourself.

Money mirrors the stories you tell yourself when no one else is listening. It echoes beliefs about what you deserve, what is possible, and how safe the world feels to you. If scarcity dominates your thoughts, the mirror reflects fear; if worthiness feels conditional, the mirror reflects instability. The numbers themselves are neutral, but the meaning assigned to them determines the emotional response.

Seeing money as a mirror allows curiosity to replace self-attack. Instead of asking "What's wrong with me?" the question becomes "What is this showing me?" This shift transforms money from a weapon into an informant. Awareness begins when reflection replaces reaction.

How Identity Gets Entangled with Numbers

Identity entanglement happens quietly, often through repetition rather than trauma alone. Statements like "I'm bad with money" or "People like me never get ahead" are absorbed and reinforced through experience. Over time, these beliefs harden into self-concepts, shaping decisions and expectations before conscious choice enters the picture. Money becomes proof of an identity rather than a temporary condition.

Cultural conditioning intensifies this entanglement by equating financial success with moral virtue. Wealth is praised as discipline and intelligence, while struggle is framed as irresponsibility or failure. These narratives ignore structural realities and place the burden of explanation on the individual. When identity absorbs these messages, self-worth becomes externally adjustable.

Once identity is tied to money, emotional volatility increases. Confidence rises and falls with income, creating an unstable sense of self. Even financial gains may not bring peace, because the identity remains dependent on maintaining the number. This dependence turns money into an emotional regulator instead of a neutral tool.

Untangling identity from numbers does not mean rejecting ambition or responsibility. It means restoring proportion. Money can influence comfort and options, but it does not define character, intelligence, or value. When identity is reclaimed, money loses its power to dictate self-perception.

What Your Bank Account Is Actually Showing You

A bank account reflects patterns, not worth. It shows habits, access, timing, and decisions made within specific constraints. It may also reflect emotional coping strategies such as avoidance, impulsivity, or hyper-control. None of these are moral failures; they are adaptive responses formed under pressure.

The balance also reflects inherited narratives. Family beliefs about money, survival, generosity, or fear often operate beneath awareness. These narratives shape behavior automatically, long before logic intervenes. Recognizing these influences reveals that many financial patterns were learned, not chosen.

Your account may be reflecting periods of illness, caregiving, burnout, or systemic barriers. These realities are frequently erased in self-judgment, replaced by harsh internal explanations. Seeing the full context restores fairness to the interpretation. A mirror without context distorts the image.

When viewed accurately, the bank account becomes data rather than a verdict. Data invites adjustment; verdicts invite shame. Learning to read the reflection without condemnation creates space for intentional change rather than emotional paralysis.

Reclaiming the Self Behind the Reflection

Reclaiming the self begins with separating observation from identity. You can observe your financial reality without merging with it. This distinction creates emotional distance, allowing clearer thinking and kinder self-assessment. Awareness without fusion is the foundation of healing.

As identity loosens its grip on money, self-trust begins to rebuild. Decisions are no longer driven solely by fear or compensation. Instead, they are guided by values, needs, and long-term stability. This shift transforms how money is used and experienced.

Reclaiming the self also restores dignity. You are no longer required to justify your existence through productivity or accumulation. Worth becomes inherent rather than earned. From this place, financial growth becomes supportive rather than defining.

When the self is no longer trapped in the mirror, money resumes its proper role. It becomes a resource, not a ruler. The reflection remains, but it no longer decides who you are.

Exercise 1: Identifying the Reflection

Step 1: Write down your current bank balance without adding commentary or emotion.

Step 2: List the first five thoughts or feelings that arise when you see this number.

Step 3: For each thought, ask whether it describes a fact or a belief about yourself.

Exercise 2: Separating Identity from Data

Step 1: Write the sentence "My bank account says ___ about me" and complete it honestly.

Step 2: Rewrite the sentence as "My bank account reflects ___ circumstances or patterns."

Step 3: Notice how your body responds to each version and record the difference.

Exercise 3: Context Restoration

Step 1: List three life factors that have influenced your financial situation beyond effort alone.

Step 2: Acknowledge how each factor shaped decisions or limitations at the time.

Step 3: Write one sentence of compassion toward yourself for navigating those conditions.

Money Trauma Healing Tip

Money trauma often lives in the nervous system, not the intellect. When financial thoughts trigger anxiety, slow your breathing before engaging the numbers. Regulating the body creates safety, allowing clearer interpretation of the reflection. Healing begins when the body learns that numbers are not threats.

Beyond Money Tip

Your identity existed before your first paycheck and will exist beyond any balance. Spend time investing in self-definition through values, creativity, and presence. These anchors remain stable regardless of financial fluctuation. A grounded self makes wiser choices naturally.

Journal Prompts

1. What did money symbolize in my early environment?
2. When did I first feel judged by a number?
3. What beliefs about money feel inherited rather than chosen?
4. How do I treat myself differently when my balance is higher or lower?
5. What parts of my identity have nothing to do with money?
6. How do fear and safety show up in my financial decisions?
7. What would change if money stopped being a measure of worth?
8. How does my body react to financial stress?
9. What compassion does my financial story deserve?
10. Who am I when numbers are removed from the equation?

Closing Reflection

Money can only reflect what stands before it. When identity is placed in the mirror, the reflection becomes heavy and distorted. As you reclaim the self behind the numbers, the mirror loses its authority and gains clarity. This chapter marks the beginning of seeing yourself directly—without distortion, without judgment, and without needing a number to confirm your worth.

Chapter 2: When Balance Sheets Shape Self-Worth

The Quiet Equation Between Worth and Wealth

Self-worth often becomes tied to financial metrics through repetition rather than choice. Over time, balances, credit limits, and income figures begin to feel like evidence of personal value. This equation forms quietly, reinforced each time success is praised in monetary terms or struggle is dismissed as a personal flaw. Eventually, the mind stops questioning the equation and accepts it as truth.

Once worth is measured financially, the internal landscape becomes unstable. Confidence inflates with gains and collapses with losses, creating an emotional dependency on numbers that were never designed to carry that weight. This volatility is exhausting, yet normalized in cultures that reward output over presence. The result is a self-concept that feels perpetually conditional.

Balance sheets appear objective, but the interpretation is deeply emotional. Two people can look at the same number and experience entirely different internal responses based on belief, history, and comparison. The worth equation is not built on math alone; it is built on meaning layered over math. That meaning is learned, not innate.

Recognizing this equation is an act of liberation. When you see how worth has been outsourced to numbers, you regain the ability to question the contract. Awareness loosens the grip of the balance sheet and opens space for a more stable sense of self to emerge.

How External Metrics Override Internal Value

External metrics gain power when internal value is underdeveloped or repeatedly invalidated. Praise becomes transactional, offered when output is visible and withheld when it is not. Over time, the nervous system learns to seek safety through measurable performance. Money becomes a shorthand for approval.

This override disconnects people from intrinsic worth. Effort that does not immediately translate into income is dismissed, even when it builds skills, resilience, or healing. Rest becomes guilt-ridden, creativity becomes justified only when profitable, and presence feels unproductive. The inner world is gradually deprioritized.

When internal value is overridden, comparison intensifies. Others' financial milestones are internalized as personal failures. Social media, pay transparency, and curated success stories amplify this effect, creating constant reference points. The self becomes reactive, scanning for evidence of adequacy or inadequacy.

Restoring internal value requires conscious re-centering. It means learning to validate effort, intention, and growth without waiting for external confirmation. When internal value is restored, external metrics lose their power to dictate self-worth.

The Emotional Cost of Living by the Numbers

Living by the numbers extracts a quiet but persistent emotional cost. Anxiety becomes chronic, tied to fluctuations that feel personal and threatening. Even stability can feel fragile, as the fear of loss overshadows the experience of sufficiency. Peace is postponed until a future number is reached.

Shame often accompanies this lifestyle, especially during downturns. Instead of viewing financial difficulty as a circumstance, it is internalized as a character flaw. This shame isolates, discouraging transparency and support. Silence becomes another cost of the equation.

Over-identification with numbers also narrows identity. Qualities like kindness, creativity, and resilience are overshadowed by financial performance. Life becomes smaller, defined by spreadsheets rather than lived experience. The richness of being is traded for the illusion of control.

Acknowledging the emotional cost allows recalibration. Numbers can inform decisions without dictating worth. When emotional well-being is prioritized alongside financial responsibility, balance becomes possible without self-erasure.

Redefining Worth Beyond the Ledger

Redefining worth begins with disentangling evaluation from existence. You can evaluate finances without evaluating yourself. This distinction restores dignity and reduces emotional reactivity. It allows for honest assessment without self-punishment.

Worth beyond the ledger is rooted in consistency, integrity, and presence. These qualities persist regardless of financial fluctuation. When they become the reference point, self-respect stabilizes. Money becomes a variable rather than a verdict.

This redefinition also shifts motivation. Actions are taken from alignment rather than fear. Growth becomes sustainable because it is not driven by self-rejection. The nervous system relaxes, improving clarity and decision-making.

Living beyond the ledger does not mean ignoring numbers; it means contextualizing them. Financial awareness paired with intrinsic worth creates resilience. From this place, both stability and expansion are possible.

Exercise 1: Identifying the Worth Equation

Step 1: Write down the financial number that most affects your mood.

Step 2: Complete the sentence "When this number changes, it means I am ___."

Step 3: Question whether this meaning is factual or learned.

Exercise 2: Internal Value Inventory

Step 1: List five qualities you possess that exist independent of money.

Step 2: Describe one way each quality has supported you through difficulty.

Step 3: Reflect on how often these qualities go unacknowledged.

Exercise 3: Reframing Financial Evaluation

Step 1: Review your current financial situation as if assessing a project, not a person.

Step 2: Note what adjustments are practical without attaching judgment.

Step 3: Write one supportive statement you would offer someone else in the same position.

Money Trauma Healing Tip

If financial numbers trigger self-criticism, pause and ground your attention in the body. Place a hand on your chest and breathe slowly until tension decreases. This interrupts the shame response and restores safety. Self-worth cannot be rebuilt in a state of threat.

Beyond Money Tip

Practice naming moments of value that have nothing to do with productivity. Notice when presence, patience, or honesty shape your day. These moments reinforce intrinsic worth. Over time, they become a more reliable foundation than numbers.

Journal Prompts

1. When did I first link money with worth?
2. Whose approval do financial numbers represent for me?
3. How does my body respond to financial comparison?
4. What parts of me have been ignored in favor of numbers?
5. How do I speak to myself during financial stress?
6. What would self-respect look like without financial proof?
7. How has shame influenced my financial choices?
8. What internal values deserve recognition today?
9. How would I define success without money?
10. What changes when worth becomes intrinsic?

Closing Reflection

Balance sheets were never meant to carry the weight of identity. When self-worth is outsourced to numbers, the self becomes fragile and reactive. By reclaiming value beyond the ledger, you restore stability and dignity to your inner world. This chapter invites you to let numbers inform your life—without letting them define you.

Chapter 3: Detaching Identity from Dollar Signs

How Identity Becomes Financially Branded

Identity does not attach itself to money overnight; it is branded slowly through repetition, reinforcement, and emotional imprinting. Each time approval follows financial success, or shame follows financial difficulty, the mind records a lesson about who you are allowed to be. Over years, these lessons accumulate into an unspoken rule: *I am what my numbers say I am*. This branding feels natural because it is familiar, not because it is true.

Once branded, identity begins to self-police. You may hesitate to rest, create, or speak confidently unless the numbers justify it. Financial stress becomes personal rather than situational, and ambition turns into self-correction rather than self-expression. The brand tightens most during instability, when fear demands a quick explanation and identity becomes the easiest target.

This branding also limits possibility. When identity is tied to income level, growth feels risky because failure threatens the self, not just the strategy. Opportunities are filtered through fear of what a result might "say" about you. The dollar sign becomes a gatekeeper to confidence, belonging, and permission.

Recognizing financial branding is not about blame; it is about clarity. You did not choose to be branded this way—you were trained. Awareness loosens the label and creates the space necessary to choose a different foundation for identity.

Why Detachment Feels Uncomfortable at First

Detaching identity from money often triggers discomfort because the nervous system equates familiarity with safety. Even painful patterns can feel stabilizing when they are predictable. When money has long served as an identity anchor, removing it can feel like floating without orientation. This unease is a signal of transition, not danger.

Many people mistake this discomfort for irresponsibility or denial. In reality, detachment does not mean ignoring finances; it means refusing to let them define the self. The discomfort arises because the mind is recalibrating its reference point. Old equations are dissolving, and new ones have not yet solidified.

Fear may surface in subtle ways—over-checking balances, seeking reassurance, or mentally rehearsing worst-case scenarios. These behaviors are attempts to restore the old identity structure. Observing them without judgment accelerates the detachment process. Resistance fades when safety is reestablished internally.

Detachment becomes easier as self-trust grows. When you learn that identity remains intact regardless of financial fluctuation, the nervous system relaxes. What once felt destabilizing becomes freeing.

Building a Non-Financial Sense of Self

A non-financial sense of self is built through consistent recognition of intrinsic qualities. These include values, character, creativity, adaptability, and presence—traits that persist independent of income. Naming and honoring these traits strengthens identity from the inside out. This internal anchoring reduces emotional dependence on external metrics.

This process requires repetition, especially in moments of stress. When money pressure arises, consciously reaffirming non-financial identity interrupts old reflexes. Over time, the mind learns that worth is stable, even when circumstances are not. Stability becomes internal rather than conditional.

Relationships also shift as non-financial identity strengthens. Interactions become less performative and more authentic. You are no longer required to prove value through productivity or success. Connection deepens when presence replaces performance.

A self built beyond money is resilient. It can pursue growth without self-erasure and endure setbacks without collapse. This resilience is not passive; it is actively cultivated through awareness and choice.

Reclaiming Agency Without Self-Definition

Agency returns when money is removed from the role of identity authority. You regain the ability to make decisions based on alignment rather than self-judgment. Choices become strategic instead of defensive. This shift restores creativity and flexibility.

Without identity attached, financial outcomes become information rather than affirmation. You can adjust, experiment, and refine without interpreting results as personal verdicts. Progress accelerates because energy is no longer spent protecting the self from perceived failure.

Reclaimed agency also brings compassion. You can acknowledge mistakes without self-condemnation and successes without inflation. Balance replaces extremes. The emotional charge around money softens, making space for clearer action.

Detaching identity from dollar signs does not reduce ambition; it purifies it. Goals become expressions of desire rather than attempts at self-validation. From this place, both peace and progress coexist.

Exercise 1: Identifying Identity Hooks

Step 1: Write three statements you commonly associate with money and yourself (examples: "I'm behind," "I'm successful," "I'm irresponsible").

Step 2: For each statement, underline the word that defines *you* rather than the situation.

Step 3: Rewrite each statement so it describes circumstances without labeling identity.

Exercise 2: Building Non-Financial Anchors

Step 1: List five qualities that describe who you are at your best, excluding anything related to money or productivity.

Step 2: For each quality, write one recent example of it showing up in your life.

Step 3: Create a single sentence that defines your identity using only these qualities.

Exercise 3: Practicing Detachment in Real Time

Step 1: Recall a recent financial stress moment and write what you believed it said about you.

Step 2: Separate the fact from the interpretation by listing them on two different lines.

Step 3: Write a grounded response you would give yourself if identity were not at stake.

Money Trauma Healing Tip

When identity detachment triggers anxiety, slow the process intentionally. Place one hand on your chest and one on your abdomen while breathing steadily. This signals safety to the nervous system and reduces the urge to self-define through numbers. Calm creates clarity.

Beyond Money Tip

Choose one daily action that affirms identity without productivity—such as rest, creativity, or honest conversation. These acts reinforce intrinsic worth. Over time, they weaken the reflex to seek validation through outcomes. Identity grows stronger through presence.

Journal Prompts

1. When did I first feel defined by money?
2. What fears arise when I imagine separating worth from income?
3. How does my body react when I check financial numbers?
4. What parts of me remain constant regardless of money?
5. How has money shaped my self-talk?
6. What would freedom from financial identity feel like?
7. Who am I when no one is measuring me?
8. How do I treat myself during financial uncertainty?
9. What values do I want my identity rooted in?
10. What changes when money stops being a mirror of worth?

Closing Reflection

Detaching identity from dollar signs is not a loss—it is a return. When money no longer speaks for who you are, silence reveals something steadier beneath the noise. This chapter marks the shift from borrowed definitions to chosen truth. You are not what you earn, hold, or owe—you are what remains when the numbers are stripped away.

Chapter 4: Building a Values-Based Self

Why Values Create Stability Where Money Cannot

Money fluctuates by design, but values endure by choice. When identity is rooted in financial outcomes, self-perception rises and falls with forces often outside personal control. Values, by contrast, remain accessible regardless of circumstance. They provide an internal structure that holds steady when external systems shift.

A values-based self offers continuity. Even in periods of financial uncertainty, values such as integrity, curiosity, compassion, or perseverance continue to guide behavior. This continuity reduces emotional volatility and restores a sense of reliability within the self. Stability becomes internal rather than conditional.

When values are unclear or unclaimed, money fills the vacuum. Numbers begin to dictate decisions, boundaries, and self-respect because nothing else has been named as authoritative. Clarifying values removes this dependency. The self no longer needs financial proof to feel grounded.

Building identity around values does not minimize ambition. Instead, it refines it. Goals become aligned with what matters most rather than driven by fear, comparison, or compensation. Purpose replaces pressure.

Identifying Values That Are Truly Yours

Many people believe they know their values, but what they often hold are inherited priorities. Cultural conditioning, family survival strategies, and social expectations frequently masquerade as personal values. These borrowed standards feel heavy because they were never consciously chosen. Differentiating them is essential to building an authentic self.

True values generate energy rather than depletion. When actions align with genuine values, effort feels meaningful even when challenging. When actions align with borrowed values, exhaustion and resentment follow. This emotional feedback is a reliable indicator of authenticity.

Identifying true values requires honest reflection. It involves noticing moments of pride, peace, or quiet satisfaction that arise independent of recognition or reward. These moments point toward what matters most internally. Values reveal themselves through experience more than ideals.

Once identified, values serve as internal reference points. Decisions can be evaluated by alignment rather than outcome alone. This reduces regret and strengthens self-trust, even when results are imperfect.

Living from Values Instead of Validation

Validation seeks approval; values seek expression. When identity depends on validation, actions become performative. Choices are shaped by how they will be perceived rather than whether they are aligned. This creates chronic tension and self-monitoring.

Living from values shifts motivation inward. Actions are taken because they reflect who you choose to be, not because they guarantee praise or profit. This internal motivation is more sustainable and less reactive. Confidence becomes quieter but steadier.

This shift also changes how success is measured. Success becomes fidelity to values rather than external metrics alone. A day lived in alignment is considered successful even if it lacks visible achievement. This reframing reduces pressure and increases fulfillment.

Over time, living from values builds integrity. Words, actions, and self-perception align. This integrity strengthens identity, making it less vulnerable to financial fluctuation or external judgment.

Integrating Values into Daily Decisions

Values become real through practice, not declaration. Integration happens in small, consistent choices rather than grand gestures. How you speak to yourself, set boundaries, and allocate attention are daily expressions of values. These choices compound over time.

Financial decisions also shift under values-based identity. Spending, saving, and earning are guided by alignment rather than fear or compensation. Money becomes a servant of values rather than a substitute for them. This creates coherence between inner and outer life.

Integration requires self-awareness during stress. Old habits may resurface under pressure, tempting a return to validation-seeking. Gentle redirection rather than self-criticism maintains progress. Values strengthen through patience.

A values-based self is adaptable. It can navigate change without losing orientation. When values lead, identity remains intact even as circumstances evolve.

Exercise 1: Clarifying Core Values

Step 1: Write down ten words that feel meaningful to how you want to live (examples: honesty, freedom, creativity, care, courage).

Step 2: Narrow the list to five by asking which values you would keep if external rewards were removed.

Step 3: For each of the final five values, write one sentence describing what it looks like in daily behavior.

Exercise 2: Detecting Borrowed Values

Step 1: List three expectations you feel pressured to meet, especially around money or success.

Step 2: For each expectation, ask whether it energizes or drains you.

Step 3: Rewrite one draining expectation as a value-aligned alternative that feels authentic.

Exercise 3: Values-Based Decision Practice

Step 1: Recall a recent decision you made primarily for approval or security.

Step 2: Identify which value was compromised or ignored in that decision.

Step 3: Describe how the decision could have looked if guided by that value instead.

Money Trauma Healing Tip

When financial stress challenges your values, slow down before acting. Pausing interrupts fear-based decisions that override alignment. Returning to values restores a sense of control and dignity. Healing occurs when choice replaces compulsion.

Beyond Money Tip

Choose one value to practice intentionally each day for a week. Let it guide at least one small action daily. This repetition strengthens identity beyond outcomes. Values become lived reality through consistency.

Journal Prompts

1. Which values feel most stable in my life?
2. Where have I confused values with validation?
3. How do my values show up during stress?
4. What values feel inherited rather than chosen?
5. When do I feel most aligned with myself?
6. How do my financial choices reflect my values?
7. What would change if values led my decisions?
8. Which value needs more attention right now?
9. How does living from values affect my sense of worth?
10. What kind of person do I choose to be, regardless of money?

Closing Reflection

A values-based self does not fluctuate with income, approval, or comparison. It provides a steady ground from which to engage the world honestly and intentionally. As money releases its hold on identity, values rise to take their rightful place. This chapter marks the construction of a self that stands firm—rooted not in numbers, but in meaning.

Chapter 5: The New Mirror: Self Before Symbol

Why the Old Mirror No Longer Works

The old mirror was built from symbols—numbers, balances, scores, and external signals that promised clarity but delivered distortion. It trained you to look outward for confirmation of who you were, using money as the quickest reflection available. Over time, this mirror became familiar, even authoritative, despite its instability. What once felt informative eventually became corrosive.

That mirror no longer works because it was never designed to hold identity. Symbols shift faster than the self can safely adapt to. When meaning is outsourced to something volatile, the internal world becomes reactive rather than rooted. The exhaustion that follows is not a personal failure; it is a structural mismatch.

As awareness grows, the old mirror begins to crack. You notice how often your mood, confidence, and self-talk change in response to symbols rather than substance. This recognition signals readiness for transition. When the old mirror loses credibility, space opens for something truer.

Letting go of the old mirror is not about rejection—it is about graduation. You are no longer willing to let symbols speak louder than lived truth. What replaces it must reflect the self first.

Reclaiming the Primary Reflection

The new mirror does not live outside you. It is constructed from awareness, values, and presence rather than symbols. Instead of asking what the numbers say, you ask how aligned you are with who you choose to be. This shift restores authority to the self.

Primary reflection is quieter but more accurate. It notices effort, intention, growth, and integrity—things symbols cannot measure. When these become visible, self-recognition replaces self-surveillance. The nervous system relaxes because the reflection is no longer hostile.

This mirror reflects process rather than outcome. It honors movement, learning, and course correction without demanding perfection. Failure loses its power to define because it is no longer interpreted as identity evidence. The self remains intact throughout change.

Reclaiming the primary reflection also restores choice. You decide what matters before symbols enter the conversation. Money becomes context, not commentary.

Using Symbols Without Becoming Them

Symbols are not the enemy; misplacement is. Money, metrics, and milestones can be useful when they are secondary to self-knowledge. In the new mirror, symbols are tools rather than judges. They inform decisions without issuing verdicts.

Using symbols consciously requires boundaries. You choose when to look and how to interpret what you see. This prevents emotional hijacking and reactive behavior. Symbols lose their power to destabilize because they no longer define meaning.

This relationship creates emotional neutrality. Wins are appreciated without inflation; losses are addressed without collapse. Perspective replaces panic. The self remains centered regardless of symbolic fluctuation.

When symbols are placed in their proper role, they become supportive. They serve growth rather than control it. The mirror reflects the self first—and symbols second.

Living From the New Mirror Daily

Living from the new mirror requires daily reinforcement. Old reflexes may resurface, especially during stress or comparison. Awareness rather than resistance keeps the transition steady. Each moment of choice strengthens the new orientation.

Daily life becomes less performative and more present. Decisions are guided by alignment rather than image. Rest, creativity, and honesty regain legitimacy without financial justification. The self is allowed to exist fully.

This way of living creates emotional resilience. External changes no longer threaten identity because the reflection is internal. Confidence becomes grounded rather than conditional. Stability becomes a lived experience.

Over time, the new mirror becomes automatic. You check in with yourself before checking numbers. The order matters—and it changes everything.

Exercise 1: Retiring the Old Mirror

Step 1: Write down the symbols you most often use to evaluate yourself (balances, income, status, productivity markers).

Step 2: For each symbol, note how it affects your mood and self-talk.

Step 3: Write one sentence stating what that symbol cannot accurately reflect about you.

Exercise 2: Defining the New Mirror

Step 1: List five indicators that truly reflect who you are becoming (values lived, effort shown, honesty practiced).

Step 2: Describe how each indicator feels internally when it is present.

Step 3: Create a short personal statement defining success using only these indicators.

Exercise 3: Practicing Self-First Evaluation

Step 1: At the end of a day, write one way you honored yourself independent of outcomes.

Step 2: Note one symbol you encountered that day and how you interpreted it.

Step 3: Rewrite that interpretation from the perspective of the new mirror.

Money Trauma Healing Tip

When symbols trigger old identity reactions, interrupt the habit immediately. Place attention on breath and bodily sensation before engaging the meaning. This restores safety and prevents symbolic over-identification. The body must feel safe for the new mirror to function.

Beyond Money Tip

Begin each day with a self-check before any metric check. Ask how you feel, what you need, and what matters today. This sets the hierarchy correctly. Symbols follow the self—not the other way around.

Journal Prompts

1. What symbols have defined me in the past?
2. How did those symbols distort my self-view?
3. What does my inner mirror reflect today?
4. When do I feel most aligned with myself?
5. How do symbols influence my emotions?
6. What remains constant when numbers change?
7. How does self-first evaluation feel in my body?
8. What old mirror habits still appear?
9. What does success mean without symbols?
10. Who am I becoming beyond numbers?

Closing Reflection

The new mirror does not ask for proof—it offers presence. When the self is placed before the symbol, identity stabilizes and meaning deepens. Money returns to its proper role, and the reflection becomes clear without distortion. This is not the absence of symbols, but the restoration of order: self first, always.

Appendix A: Self-Image Reinvention Rituals

These rituals are designed to help you consciously rebuild how you see yourself—separating identity from symbols, outcomes, and external validation. Each ritual works on a different layer of self-image and should be practiced slowly, with intention. You may repeat any ritual as often as needed.

Ritual 1: The Mirror Reclamation Ritual

Purpose: To reclaim your self-image from external measures and return authority to the self.

Step 1: Stand or sit in front of a mirror in a quiet space. Look directly at yourself without adjusting posture, expression, or appearance.

Step 2: Say aloud: *"I am not a symbol. I am a self."* Repeat this three times slowly.

Step 3: Name three qualities you see in yourself that have nothing to do with money, productivity, or status. Speak them clearly.

Step 4: Place your hand over your chest and say: *"I recognize myself without numbers."* Hold eye contact for ten breaths.

Ritual 2: The Identity Unlinking Ritual

Purpose: To consciously detach self-worth from financial or performance-based identity hooks.

Step 1: Write down three statements where money or success has defined you (example: "I'm behind," "I'm only valuable when productive").

Step 2: Draw a line through each statement and rewrite it without identity language (example: "My situation is changing," "I am valuable regardless of output").

Step 3: Read the rewritten statements aloud slowly, allowing discomfort to surface without correcting it.

Step 4: End by writing: *"Identity restored to self, not symbol."* Date the page.

Ritual 3: The Self-Before-Symbol Reset

Purpose: To retrain the nervous system to check in with self before metrics.

Step 1: Choose one full day where you delay checking any financial numbers until midday.

Step 2: Before any symbol interaction, ask yourself three questions: *How do I feel? What do I need? What matters today?* Write the answers down.

Step 3: When you later check numbers, observe your emotional response without judgment.

Step 4: Conclude the day by writing one sentence about who you were that day independent of outcomes.

Ritual 4: The Values Anchoring Ritual

Purpose: To rebuild self-image around values rather than validation.

Step 1: Choose one core value that feels stabilizing (such as honesty, care, courage, or creativity).

Step 2: Write a single action you can take today that expresses this value without involving money.

Step 3: Perform the action consciously, noticing how it feels in your body and mind.

Step 4: Record the experience and write: *"This is who I am when values lead."*

Ritual 5: The Compassionate Reframing Ritual

Purpose: To soften self-judgment linked to past financial experiences.

Step 1: Write about a financial moment that still affects how you see yourself. Be factual, not critical.

Step 2: List three contextual factors that influenced this moment (health, timing, knowledge, environment, pressure).

Step 3: Write a compassionate statement you would offer someone else in the same situation.

Step 4: Read that statement aloud to yourself and end with: *"I release identity from this moment."*

Ritual 6: The New Self Image Declaration
Purpose: To consciously install a new internal definition of self.

Step 1: Write a paragraph beginning with *"I am a person who..."* using only intrinsic qualities, values, and ways of being.

Step 2: Read the paragraph aloud slowly, noticing any resistance or emotion without correcting it.

Step 3: Rewrite the paragraph once more, simplifying it into three clear sentences.

Step 4: Sign and date the declaration as a commitment to self-defined identity.

Closing Reflection

Self-image is not rebuilt through force, affirmation, or denial—it is rebuilt through repetition, safety, and choice. Each ritual in this appendix exists to gently return authority to where it belongs: within you. As you practice these exercises, notice how the urgency to prove, justify, or explain yourself begins to soften. That softening is not weakness; it is integration.

Reinvention does not mean becoming someone new. It means uncovering who you were before symbols, numbers, and external measures were asked to carry your identity. With each ritual, the mirror grows clearer, and the reflection grows steadier. Over time, you may find that self-recognition arrives before self-judgment—and that is the true sign of change.

Carry these rituals forward not as tasks to complete, but as anchors you can return to whenever the old mirrors try to reclaim authority. The self you are building does not fluctuate with circumstance. It remains—quiet, grounded, and intact—long after the symbols fade.

Appendix B: Identity Inventory Exercise

This exercise is designed to help you take a full, honest inventory of who you are—separate from money, roles, outcomes, and external validation. It is not meant to be rushed. Return to it periodically as your self-concept evolves. Identity becomes clearer when it is observed without pressure to perform or prove.

Part I: Clearing the Surface Noise

Purpose: To separate identity from labels that have accumulated through circumstance and expectation.

Step 1: Write down every label you regularly use to describe yourself, both positive and negative (examples: successful, behind, responsible, struggling, reliable, disappointing).

Step 2: Circle the labels that are tied to outcomes, productivity, or money.

Step 3: Cross out those labels and write next to each one: *"This describes a situation, not my being."*

Part II: Identifying Core Traits

Purpose: To uncover stable aspects of self that persist across changing conditions.

Step 1: List ten traits that have shown up repeatedly throughout your life, regardless of success or failure (examples: persistence, curiosity, sensitivity, adaptability, loyalty).

Step 2: Narrow the list to five by identifying which traits have remained present even during your hardest periods.

Step 3: For each of the five traits, write one memory that proves its presence.

Part III: Mapping Values to Behavior

Purpose: To align identity with lived values rather than aspirational ideals.

Step 1: Write down five values that feel most meaningful to you right now.

Step 2: For each value, list one way it has shown up in your actual behavior within the last month.

Step 3: Notice which values are lived consistently and which feel more aspirational, without judgment.

Part IV: Separating Self from Roles

Purpose: To loosen identity attachment to roles that can change or disappear.

Step 1: List all the roles you occupy (examples: worker, caregiver, creator, partner, survivor).

Step 2: Write one sentence describing who you are when each role is removed.

Step 3: Underline the words that repeat across multiple role-free descriptions.

Part V: Reclaiming the Internal Definition

Purpose: To consciously define identity from the inside rather than through external reference.

Step 1: Using everything uncovered in the previous sections, write a paragraph beginning with *"At my core, I am..."*

Step 2: Remove any words that reference money, status, achievement, or comparison.

Step 3: Read the paragraph aloud and notice what feels grounded versus forced.

Part VI: Installing the Inventory

Purpose: To integrate the identity inventory into daily awareness.

Step 1: Choose one sentence from your inventory that feels stabilizing.

Step 2: Write it somewhere visible or repeat it internally during moments of stress.

Step 3: Revisit this appendix monthly and revise as your self-understanding deepens.

Closing Reflection

Identity is not something you earn, prove, or maintain through effort—it is something you recognize and protect. This inventory reveals what remains when circumstances shift and symbols lose authority. The more familiar you become with this internal landscape, the less power external measures hold over your sense of self.

Return to this exercise whenever confusion, comparison, or self-doubt resurfaces. Each time you do, the definition of who you are becomes clearer, steadier, and more self-directed. This is not the end of identity work, but a foundation—one built not on numbers or narratives, but on truth.

Message from the Author:

I hope you enjoyed this book, I love astrology and knew there was not a book such as this out on the shelf. I love metaphysical items as well. Please check out my other books:

-Life of Government Benefits

-My life of Hell

-My life with Hydrocephalus

-Red Sky

-World Domination:Woman's rule

-World Domination:Woman's Rule 2: The War

-Life and Banishment of Apophis: book 1

-The Kidney Friendly Diet

-The Ultimate Hemp Cookbook

-Creating a Dispensary(legally)

-Cleanliness throughout life: the importance of showering from childhood to adulthood.

-Strong Roots: The Risks of Overcoddling children

-Hemp Horoscopes: Cosmic Insights and Earthly Healing

- Celestial Hemp Navigating the Zodiac: Through the Green Cosmos

-Astrological Hemp: Aligning The Stars with Earth's Ancient Herb

-The Astrological Guide to Hemp: Stars, Signs, and Sacred Leaves

-Green Growth: Innovative Marketing Strategies for your Hemp Products and Dispensary

-Cosmic Cannabis

-Astrological Munchies

-Henry The Hemp

-Zodiacal Roots: The Astrological Soul Of Hemp

- **Green Constellations: Intersection of Hemp and Zodiac**

-Hemp in The Houses: An astrological Adventure Through The Cannabis Galaxy

-Galactic Ganja Guide

Heavenly Hemp

Zodiac Leaves

Doctor Who Astrology

Cannastrology

Stellar Satvias and Cosmic Indicas

Celestial Cannabis: A Zodiac Journey

AstroHerbology: The Sky and The Soil: Volume 1

AstroHerbology:Celestial Cannabis:Volume 2

Cosmic Cannabis Cultivation

The Starry Guide to Herbal Harmony: Volume 1

The Starry Guide to Herbal Harmony: Cannabis Universe: Volume 2

Yugioh Astrology: Astrological Guide to Deck, Duels and more

Nightmare Mansion: Echoes of The Abyss

Nightmare Mansion 2: Legacy of Shadows

Nightmare Mansion 3: Shadows of the Forgotten

Nightmare Mansion 4: Echoes of the Damned

The Life and Banishment of Apophis: Book 2

Nightmare Mansion: Halls of Despair

Healing with Herb: Cannabis and Hydrocephalus

Planetary Pot: Aligning with Astrological Herbs: Volume 1

Fast Track to Freedom: 30 Days to Financial Independence Using AI, Assets, and Agile Hustles

Cosmic Hemp Pathways

How to Become Financially Free in 30 Days: 10,000 Paths to Prosperity

Zodiacal Herbage: Astrological Insights: Volume 1

Nightmare Mansion: Whispers in the Walls

The Daleks Invade Atlantis

Henry the hemp and Hydrocephalus

10X The Kidney Friendly Diet

Cannabis Universe: Adult coloring book

Hemp Astrology: The Healing Power of the Stars

Zodiacal Herbage: Astrological Insights: Cannabis Universe: Volume 2

Planetary Pot: Aligning with Astrological Herbs: Cannabis Universes: Volume 2

Doctor Who: Convergence Protocol – The Replicator War

Nightmare Mansion: Curse of the Blood Moon

The Celestial Stoner: A Guide to the Zodiac

Cosmic Pleasures: Sex Toy Astrology for Every Sign

Hydrocephalus Astrology: Navigating the Stars and Healing Waters

Lapis and the Mischievous Chocolate Bar

Celestial Positions: Sexual Astrology for Every Sign

Apophis's Shadow Work Journal: **:** A Journey of Self-Discovery and Healing

Kinky Cosmos: Sexual Kink Astrology for Every Sign

Digital Cosmos: The Astrological Digimon Compendium

Stellar Seeds: The Cosmic Guide to Growing with Astrology

Apophis's Daily Gratitude Journal

Cat Astrology: Feline Mysteries of the Cosmos

The Cosmic Kama Sutra: An Astrological Guide to Sexual Positions

Unleash Your Potential: A Guided Journal Powered by AI Insights

Whispers of the Enchanted Grove

Cosmic Pleasures: An Astrological Guide to Sexual Kinks

369, 12 Manifestation Journal

Whisper of the nocturne journal(blank journal for writing or drawing)

The Boogey Book

Locked In Reflection: A Chastity Journey Through Locktober

Generating Wealth Quickly:How to Generate $100,000 in 24 Hours

Star Magic: Harness the Power of the Universe

The Flatulence Chronicles: A Fart Journal for Self-Discovery

The Doctor and The Death Moth

Seize the Day: A Personal Seizure Tracking Journal

The Ultimate Boogeyman Safari: A Journey into the Boogie World and Beyond

Whispers of Samhain: 1,000 Spells of Love, Luck, and Lunar Magic: Samhain Spell Book

Apophis's guides:Witch's Spellbook Crafting Guide for Halloween

Frost & Flame: The Enchanted Yule Grimoire of 1000 Winter Spells

The Ultimate Boogey Goo Guide & Spooky Activities for Halloween Fun

Harmony of the Scales: A Libra's Spellcraft for Balance and Beauty

The Enchanted Advent: 36 Days of Christmas Wonders

Nightmare Mansion: The Labyrinth of Screams

Harvest of Enchantment: 1,000 Spells of Gratitude, Love, and Fortune for Thanksgiving

The Boogey Chronicles: A Journal of Nightly Encounters and Shadowy Secrets

The 12 Days of Financial Freedom: A Step-by-Step Christmas Countdown to Transform Your Finances

Sigil of the Eternal Spiral Blank Journal

A Christmas Feast: Timeless Recipes for Every Meal

Holiday Stress-Free Solutions: A Survival Guide to Thriving During the Festive Season

Yu-Gi-Oh! Holiday Gifting Mastery: The Ultimate Guide for Fans and Newcomers Alike

Holiday Harmony: A Hydrocephalus Survival Guide for the Festive Season

Celestial Craft: The Witch's Almanac for 2025 – A Cosmic Guide to Manifestations, Moons, and Mystical Events

Doctor Who: The Toymaker's Winter Wonderland

Tulsa King Unveiled: A Thrilling Guide to Stallone's Mafia Masterpiece

Pendulum Craft: A Complete Guide to Crafting and Using Personalized Divination Tools

Nightmare Mansion: Santa's Eternal Eve

Starlight Noel: A Cosmic Journey through Christmas Mysteries

The Dark Architect: Unlocking the Blueprint of Existence

Surviving the Embrace: The Ultimate Guide to Encounters with The Hugging Molly

The Enchanted Codex: Secrets of the Craft for Witches, Wiccans, and Pagans

Harvest of Gratitude: A Complete Thanksgiving Guide

Yuletide Essentials: A Complete Guide to an Authentic and Magical Christmas

Celestial Smokes: A Cosmic Guide to Cigars and Astrology

Living in Balance: A Comprehensive Survival Guide to Thriving with Diabetes Insipidus

Cosmic Symbiosis: The Venom Zodiac Chronicles

The Cursed Paw of Ambition

Cosmic Symbiosis: The Astrological Venom Journal

Celestial Wonders Unfold: A Stargazer's Guide to the Cosmos (2024-2029)

The Ultimate Black Friday Prepper's Guide: Mastering Shopping Strategies and Savings

Cosmic Sales: The Astrological Guide to Black Friday Shopping

Legends of the Corn Mother and Other Harvest Myths

Whispers of the Harvest: The Corn Mother's Journal

The Evergreen Spellbook

The Doctor Meets the Boogeyman

The White Witch of Rose Hall's SpellBook

The Gingerbread Golem's Shadow: A Study in Sweet Darkness

The Gingerbread Golem Codex: An Academic Exploration of Sweet Myths

The Gingerbread Golem Grimoire: Sweet Magicks and Spells for the Festive Witch

The Curse of the Gingerbread Golem

10-minute Christmas Crafts for kids

Christmas Crisis Solutions: The Ultimate Last-Minute Survival Guide

Gingerbread Golem Recipes: Holiday Treats with a Magical Twist

The Infinite Key: Unlocking Mystical Secrets of the Ages

Enchanted Yule: A Wiccan and Pagan Guide to a Magical and Memorable Season

Dinosaurs of Power: Unlocking Ancient Magick

Astro-Dinos: The Cosmic Guide to Prehistoric Wisdom

Gallifrey's Yule Logs: A Festive Doctor Who Cookbook

The Dino Grimoire: Secrets of Prehistoric Magick

The Gift They Never Knew They Needed

The Gingerbread Golem's Culinary Alchemy: Enchanting Recipes for a Sweetly Dark Feast

A Time Lord Christmas: Holiday Adventures with the Doctor

Krampusproofing Your Home: Defensive Strategies for Yule

Silent Frights: A Collection of Christmas Creepypastas to Chill Your Bones

Santa Raptor's Jolly Carnage: A Dino-Claus Christmas Tale

Prehistoric Palettes: A Dino Wicca Coloring Journey

The Christmas Wishkeeper Chronicles

The Starlight Sleigh: A Holiday Journey

Elf Secrets: The True Magic of the North Pole

Candy Cane Conjurations

Cooking with Kids: Recipes Under 20 Minutes

Doctor Who: The TARDIS Confiscation

The Anxiety First Aid Kit: Quick Tools to Calm Your Mind

Frosty Whispers: A Winter's Tale

The Infinite Key: Unlocking the Secrets to Prosperity, Resilience, and Purpose

The Grasping Void: Why You'll Regret This Purchase

Astrology for Busy Bees: Star Signs Simplified

The Instant Focus Formula: Cut Through the Noise

The Secret Language of Colors: Unlocking the Emotional Codes

Sacred Fossil Chronicles: Blank Journal

The Christmas Cottage Miracle

Feeding Frenzy: Graboid-Inspired Recipes

Manifest in Minutes: The Quick Law of Attraction Guide

The Symbiote Chronicles: Doctor Who's Venomous Journey

Think Tiny, Grow Big: The Minimalist Mindset

The Energy Key: Unlocking Limitless Motivation

New Year, New Magic: Manifesting Your Best Year Yet

Unstoppable You: Mastering Confidence in Minutes

Infinite Energy: The Secret to Never Feeling Drained

Lightning Focus: Mastering the Art of Productivity in a Distracted World

Saturnalia Manifestation Magick: A Guide to Unlocking Abundance During the Solstice

Graboids and Garland: The Ultimate Tremors-Themed Christmas Guide

12 Nights of Holiday Magic

The Power of Pause: 60-Second Mindfulness Practices

The Quick Reset: How to Reclaim Your Life After Burnout

The Shadow Eater: A Tale of Despair and Survival

The Micro-Mastery Method: Transform Your Skills in Just Minutes a Day

Reclaiming Time: How to Live More by Doing Less
Chronovore: The Eternal Nexus
The Mind Reset: Unlocking Your Inner Peace in a Chaotic World
Confidence Code: Building Unshakable Self-Belief
Baby the Vampire Terrier
Baby the Vampire Terrier's Christmas Adventure
Celestial Streams: The Content Creator's Astrology Manual
The Wealth Whisperer: Unlocking Abundance with Everyday Actions
The Energy Equation: Maximize Your Output Without Burning Out
The Happiness Algorithm: Science-Backed Steps to Joyful Living
Stress-Free Success: Achieving Goals Without Anxiety
Mindful Wealth: The New Blueprint for Financial Freedom
The Festive Flavors of New Year: A Culinary Celebration
The Master's Gambit: Keys of Eternal Power
Shadowed Secrets: Groundhog Day Mysteries
Beneath the Burrow: Lessons from the Groundhog
Spring's Whispers: The Groundhog's Prediction
The Limitless Mindset: Unlock Your Untapped Potential
The Focus Funnel: How to Cut Through Chaos and Get Results
Bold Moves: Building Courage to Live on Your Terms
The Daily Shift: Simple Practices for Lasting Transformation
The Quarter-Life Reset: Thriving in Your 20s and 30s
The Art of Shadowplay: Building Your Own Personal Myth
The Eternal Loop: Finding Purpose in Repetition
Burrowing Wisdom: Life Lessons from the Groundhog
Shadow Work: A Groundhog Day Perspective
Love in Bloom: 5-Minute Romantic Gestures
The Shadowspell Codex: Secrets of Forbidden Magick
The Burnout Cure: Finding Balance in a Busy World
The Groundhog Prophecy: Unlocking Seasonal Secrets
Nog Tales: The Spirited History of Eggnog

Six More Weeks: Embracing Seasonal Transitions
The Lumivian Chronicles: Fragments of the Fifth Dimension
Money on Your Mind: A Beginner's Guide to Wealth
The Focus Fix: Breaking Through Distraction
January's Spirit Keepers: Mystical Protectors of the Cold
Creativity Unchained: Unlocking Your Wildest Ideas in 2025
Manifestation Mastery: 365 Days to Rewrite Your Reality
The Groundhog's Mirror: Reflecting on Change
The Weeping Angels' Christmas Curse
Burrowed in Time: A Groundhog Day Journey
Heartbeats: Poems to Share with Your Valentine
Dino Wicca: The Sacred Grimoire of Prehistoric Magick
Courage of the Pride: Finding Your Inner Roar
The Lion's Leap: Bold Moves for Big Results
Healthy Hustle: Achieving Without Overworking
Practical Manifesting: Turning Dreams into Reality in 2025
Jurassic Pharaohs: Unlocking the Magick of Ancient Egypt and Dino Wicca
The Happiness Equation: Small Changes for Big Joy
The Confidence Compass: Finding Your Inner Strength
Whispers in the Hollow: Tales of the Forgotten Beasts
Echoes from the Hollow: The Return of Forgotten Beasts
The Hollow Ascendant: The Rise of the Forgotten Beasts
The Relationship Reset: Building Better Connections
Mastering the Morning: How to Win the Day Before 8 AM
The Shadow's Dance: Groundhog Day Symbolism
Cupid's Kitchen: Quick Valentine's Day Recipes
Valentine's Day on a Budget: Love Without Breaking the Bank
Astrocraft: Aligning the Stars in the World of Minecraft
Forecasting Life: Groundhog Day Reflections
Bleeding Hearts: Twisted Tales of Valentine's Terror
Herbal Smoke Revolution: The Ultimate Guide to Nature's Cigarette Alternative

Winter's Wrath: The Complete Survival Blueprint for Extreme Freezes.

The Groundhog's Shadow: A Tale of Seasons

Burrowed Insights: Wisdom from the Groundhog

Sensual Strings: The Art of Erotic Bondage

Whispered Flames: Unlocking the Power of Fire Play

Forgotten Shadows: A Guide to Cryptids Lost to Time

Six Weeks of Secrets: Groundhog Day's Hidden Messages

Shadows and Cycles: Groundhog Day Reflections

The Art of Love Letters: Crafting the Perfect Message

Romantic Getaways at Home: Turning Your Space into Paradise

Purrfect Brews: A Cat Lover's Guide to Coffee and Companionship

The Groundhog's Wisdom: Timeless Lessons for Modern Life

The Shadow Oracle: Groundhog Day as a Predictor

Emerging from the Burrow: A Journey of Renewal

The Language of Love: Learning Your Partner's Love Style

Authorpreneur: The Ultimate Blueprint for Writing, Publishing, and Thriving as an Author

Weathering the Seasons: Groundhog Day Perspectives

Valentine's Day Magic: A Guide to Romantic Rituals

The Shadow Chronicles: Stories of Groundhog Day

Love and Laughter: Fun Games for Valentine's Day

AstroRealty: Unlocking the Stars for Property Success

The Groundhog's Path: A Guide to Seasonal Balance

Groundhog Day Diaries: Reflections in the Shadow

The Groundhog's Light: Illuminating the Path Ahead

Valentine's Traditions from Around the World

AI Wealth Revolution: Unlocking the Trillionaire Mindset

Love Rekindled: Reigniting Passion in Relationships

Single and Thriving: Self-Love on Valentine's Day

Emerald Legends: Mystical Tales of Ireland

Green Alchemy: Harnessing Nature's Magic
The Hearts of Horror: A Valentine's Day Nightmare
The Leprechaun's Guide to Wealth and Wisdom
Dancing with the Sidhe: Celebrating the Otherworld
Shamrocks and Shadows: Mysteries of the Green Isle
Emerald Energy: Harnessing Luck and Growth
The Gingerbread Golem's Valentine: A Sweetheart's Guide to Love and Enchantment
The Celtic Knot: Weaving Life and Destiny
Green Fire: Elemental Magic for St. Patrick's Day
Clover Chronicles: Finding Your Inner Luck
Ireland's Mystical Creatures: A Field Guide
Gingerbread Golem's Love Almanac
Prowl and Thrive: The Lion's Guide to Success
Love Alchemy: Transforming Your Life Through Heart Energy
WORLD DOMINATION: Woman's Rule 3:The New Life
The Midnight Rose: A Guide to Lunar Love Spells
The Forbidden Letters: Writing Your Own Love Prophecy
Luck and Lore: St. Patrick's Day for Modern Mystics
The Green Path: A Pagan Celebration of Renewal
The Dark Architect's Guide to Reprogramming Reality
Prankster's Paradise: A Guide to Harmless Hijinks
Manifest Your Reality: The Law of Attraction Simplified
The TARDIS Owner's Manual: Understanding the Doctor's Ship: *A complete guide to the TARDIS, its technology, secrets, and mysteries*
Starlit Romance: Astrology Secrets for Finding True Love
The Time Lord's Atlas: A Complete Guide to the Whoniverse: ***A breakdown of the locations, planets, and dimensions explored in Doctor Who***
Sweetheart Shadows: The Dark Side of Love and Attraction
February Fire: Reigniting Passion in Every Area of Life

The Self-Love Toolkit: 5 Ways to Embrace Who You Are
February Sparks: Ignite Your Dreams in 28 Days
March to Success: A 31-Day Action Blueprint
Ancient Paths: The 13 Sacred Principles of Dino Wicca
Echoes of Tomorrow: Navigating the AI Revolution
The Wellness Blueprint: Balancing Mind, Body, and Soul
Green Horizons: Sustainable Living for a Better Tomorrow
The AI Wealth Code: How to Make Millions with Automation
AI-Powered Creativity: Writing, Art, and Music for Profit
Extinction Rites: Rebirthing Your Soul Through Prehistoric Magick
Sacred Serpents tarot
Celestial Enchantment blank journal
Star Strains
Culinary Journeys: Exploring Global Flavors at Home
The Hollowvale Curse
The Hollowvale Harvest
The Egg of Transformation: Awakening Your Inner Power
Blooming Into Power: A Wiccan Guide to Spring Awakening
The Nightmare Nexus: The Third Doctor's Perilous Haunting
Digital Detox: Reclaiming Your Life in a Connected World
Ostara's Path: Walking the Spiral of Renewal
The Sacred Hare
Financial Freedom: Building Wealth in the Modern Age
Spring's Cauldron: Stirring the Waters of Change
The Hollowvale Pact
Quantum Consciousness: The Science of Reality Shifting
The Hollowvale Hunger
The Sacred Waters Within: A Witch's Guide to Hydrocephalus Magick
The Raven's Nest: Building a Life of Unshakable Stability
AI and the Human Mind: The Future of Intelligence
The Hollowvale Reckoning

Timeless Love: Building and Maintaining Lasting Relationships

The Raven's Roar: Unlocking Unstoppable Confidence

Raven Sight: Awakening Intuition and Inner Wisdom

The Butterfly Effect: Small Changes, Big Transformations

Taming the Boogeyman: How to Conquer Your Inner Fears

The Magick of Green: Awakening Earth's Energy in You

The Entrepreneurial Mindset: Secrets to Business Success

The Hollowvale End

The Shadow Luck Ritual: Reclaiming Power from Your Dark Side

Spring Magick for Beginners: A Simple Guide to Seasonal Energy Work

Doctor Who: The Hollowvale Conundrum

The March of Miracles: Unlocking Synchronicities in Spring

Unveiling the Cosmos: A Guide to Stargazing and Space Exploration

The Ultimate Guide to Surviving an Economic Collapse

The AI Gold Rush: How to Profit from the AI Revolution

Bastet's Shadow: The Hidden Power of Feline Magick

The Bastet Codex: Unlocking the Goddess's Magickal Secrets

Purring Spells: Harnessing Bastet's Healing Frequencies

Bastet's Nine Lives: Rebirth, Transformation, and Immortality Spells

Primal Currents: Hydrocephalus Magick in the Path of Dino Wicca

The Digital Gold Rush: Mastering E-Commerce and Online Sales

Future Shock: Adapting to the Next Decade of Change

The Quantum Mindset: Think Like a Billionaire

Sacred Motherhood: Awakening the Divine Feminine Within

The Mother's Spellbook: Enchantments for Love, Protection, and Prosperity

The Witch's Guide to Parenting: Raising Empowered and Intuitive Children

The Magick of Motherhood: Reclaiming Your Power Through Rituals

The Pagan Path to Self-Love: A Goddess's Guide to Worth and Confidence

Wild Woman Magick: Unleashing Your Primal Power

The Money Magnet Blueprint: Unlocking Unlimited Wealth

Biohacking 101: Unlock Your Body's Full Potential

The Wild Father: A Pagan Guide to Strength and Wisdom

The Sacred Masculine: Unlocking Your Inner Power

The Druid's Compass

The Warrior's Mindset

The Father's Fire

Odin's Path

Ancestral Bonds

The House That Whispers

The Magician's Code

The Wild Hunt

The Green Man's Path

The Altar of Success

The Shadow and the Sword

The High Priestess's Guide to Energy Healing

The Lunar Mother

The Sacred Self-Care Grimoire

The Womb Wisdom Codex

The Wheel of the Mother

The Witch's Guide to Manifestation

The Q2 Reset

The Ultimate Guide to AI-Powered Passive Income

Escape the 9-5

AI Feline Fortunes

The Tear-Stained Grimoire

Razorblade Runes
Cemetery Sirens
The Midnight Wristwatch
The Town That Forgets
AI Horror & Creepypasta
The Hollow Frequency
The Breach Echo
The Quiet Between Worlds
The Sigil of Tharan-Khul
Summon the Vault of Y'ha'ten
The Becoming Codex
The Profit of Az'ra-nar
The Drowned Logos
Echoes of the Eldritch Will
The Deep Ledger
Necronomicon of Networth
Covenant of the Wealthwyrm
The Whisperer's Manifesto
The Rites of Azh-K'luth
The Ark of the Crawling Coin
The Tithe of Shadows
Inkheart Abyss
The Timewinds of Y'ha-nthlei
The Spiral Labyrinth of Azag-Nirrh
The Gallifreyan Heresy of the Black Pharaoh
The Psalms of Nyog-Sotha
Black Rain Alchemy
The Infinite Maw
The Entropic Blueprint
The Oracle of Sh'guul
The Book of Breach
The Drowned Saint's Testament
Dreamcraft of the Sleeper God

The Silence Market
Cthonomics: The Dark Wealth Algorithm
Invocation of the Ten-Eyed King
Wealthbound to the Wyrm Below
Become the Unnameable
Codex of the Sovereign Flame
Rituals of Relentless Becoming
The Shadow Ascends
The Eyes Beneath You
The Will That Wakes Worlds
Silence Is a Weapon
The Mirror That Screams
The Whisper Between Moments
The Mind That Devours Fear
The Myth of the Finished Self
The Architect of Your Madness
The Voice You've Buried
The Discipline of Madness
Stormborn: Awakening Your Inner Tempest
The Mind That Ate Time
Unbind Your Becoming
The Pact You Owe Yourself
The Devourer's Diet
The Acid That Carves the Path
The Tower You Must Burn
The Breath Between Worlds
Speak Like the Deep
The Labyrinth Within
The Spine of the Sea God
Rejection Is a Portal
The Crown You Refused
The Scar Is the Spell
The Lightless Flame

The Habit of Becoming Horrific
ChickenJockey Chaos
The Gatekeeper Within
You Are Not Your Name
The Compass of the Mad
The Archive of Unsent Letters
What the Mirror Can't Show You
The Knife You Needed
Worship Nothing, Become Everything
The Other Voice
The Body the World Forgot
The Vein of the Void
The Black Bone Codex
The Puzzle of the Hidden Self (Millennium Puzzle)
The Eye That Sees the Lie *(Millennium Eye)*
The Ring of Return (Millennium Ring)
The Rod of Relentless Will ***(Millennium Rod)***
The Tally of the Soul (Millennium Tauk/Necklace)
The Key to the Locked Timeline (Millennium Key)
The Scale of Sacred Decisions (Millennium Scales)
Inferno Bites: The UnOfficial Minecraft Lava Cookbook
Rot in the Attic
Prana: The Hidden Force of Your Infinite Self
The Shadow Realm Within: Transforming Darkness Into Destiny
The Borderland Collapse
Claws of Protection: Bastet's Defensive Magick
Mr. Ring-a-Ding's Madness
Yugioh Astrology: Celestial Deckcraft and Duel Destiny (2026–2027 Edition)
The Seal You Signed: Unlocking the Power You Once Feared
The Puzzle of Infinite Minds: Unlocking the Mentalism Hidden Within

The Eye That Mirrors the All: Secrets of Inner Reflection
Doctor Who: The Toymaker's Broadcast
The Rod of Eternal Flow: Commanding the Currents of Vibration
Golden Eyes of Bastet: Enhancing Psychic Vision
The Key of Dual Forces: Balance Within the Polarity
The Scales of Living Rhythm: Timing the Dance of Life
The Necklace of Hidden Cause: Weaving the Webs of Fate
The Ring of Secret Masters: Rising Through the All Within All
Daggers of the Dying Deep
Bastet's Wealth and Fortune Magick: Prosperity Rituals of the Goddess
The Tide that Speaks
The Scrolls of Petosiris: 13 Rituals from the Feathered Eye
Petosiris and the Living Plague of Osirion
Feline Fire: Bastet's Passion and Love Magick
The Star Altar of Petosiris
Bastet's Whiskers: Supernatural Sensory Magick
The Bastet Grimoire
Feeding the Shadows
The Mouthless Prayer
The Spiral Wound
Becoming the Ibis: Lessons from Petosiris's Mind
The Crimson Coven: Cola Magick for Sweet Dominion
Sacred Cat's Paw
The Soda Zodiac: A Flavor for Every Sign
Covenant of the Crawling Flame
The Ink of Ish'Zur
Frothroot: The Thirst That Ate the World
The Golden Glyphs of Prosperity
The Etherbind Codex
Echoes of the Resistance: Reclaiming the You That Survived

Harnessed Minds: Breaking Free from Mental Control
The Eyes in the Smoke
Rootwake: The Carbon Covenant
Skitter Logic: Unlearning the Fear That Built You
Doctor Who: The World That Froths
Rootwake: The Fizz That Rewrites Flesh
Rootwake: Frothfather of the World
The Holly Pact: Blood Beneath the Mistletoe
The 2nd Mass Principle: Building Unbreakable Tribes
Web of Wits: A Survival Guide to Encounters with Anasi the Spider (Aunt Nancy)
The Hexbreaking Handbook: Effective Spells to Remove Curses
Pop Alchemy: Transform Your Life One Sip at a Time
The Mason Code: Leading in Unleadable Times
Petosiris and the Fifth Chamber of Thoth
The Ether Seed Within
The Parent of Tomorrow
Petosiris's Pyramid of Perpetual Wealth
Unlearn the World
Grimoire of the Hollow Tongue
Zodiac Weeds: Finding Your Strain Through the Stars
Aquarius Rises in the Bank
The Sugar God's Smile
The Skinclock Reversal: Biohacking the Face of Time
Debtburn: How to Obliterate What You Owe Forever
The Ice Cream Oracle: What Your Cone Says About Your Future
Silence Is Sovereignty: The Power of Being Unreadable
The Wind That Whispers Through Stone
Path of the Four Directions
Doctor Who: The Maestro's Symphony of Endings
Oxygen Grail: Breathing to Undo the Clock

Zodiacal Collapse: When Stars Devour Time
Teachings from the Red Sand Silence
Doctor Who: Omega – The Broken Equation
Memory Wipe Your Past: Start Over Like a MiB
Mitochondria Prime: Ignite the Core of Youth
A Nest of Roaches
Grub from the Galaxy: MiB Recipes You'll Never Forget
Whiskers of Power: Bastet's Guide to Inner Sovereignty
The Gift Must Cost Them: Negotiation Through Unequal Exchange
The Worm Guys' Wealth Code: Hustle Like an Alien
Bug Out: The Edgar Method for Ruthless Goal Setting
Weaving Life with Spiderwoman's Pattern
Doctor Who: The Rani's Renaissance
How to Get a Job (If You're a Puppygirl)
Speak Through Others: The Art of Proxy Power
T-Rex Your Trauma: Reclaim the Power of Your Primal Self
The Black Briefcase: How MiB Stay Wealthy in Silence
The Thirst Beyond Reason: Understanding Diabetes Insipidus From the Inside Out
Backwoods Witchcraft for Billionaires: The Pagan Path from Dirt Roads to Gold Roads
The Moonshine Grimoire: Fermented Spells for Abundance
The Nameless Geometry
The Wraith's Mixtape: Spellcasting with Songs of Sorrow
The Gallifreyan Gentleman: Silent Wealth, Sonic Confidence, and the Doctor's Code of Living
Sugar Water Confidence
Dino Totems: Spirit Guides from Earth's First Gods
Pumpkin Sigils & Ritual Smoke
The Hózhó Compass
The Distortus Discipline – Order from Inner Mutation
Witchcraft for the Cold-Blooded Soul

Moonlight Over the Blessingway
Water, Interrupted: When the Body Forgets How to Hold On
Deformed but Divine: Embracing Your Asymmetry
Hexes in the Henhouse: The Farm Witch's Guide to Power
The Reversed Flame: A Grimoire of Inverted Power
Salt, Cells, and Sanity: Reclaiming Balance with Diabetes Insipidus
King of the Broken: Crowning the Flawed Self
Moonlight Scars: Emo Moon Magick and the Art of Lunar Sorrow
Noose Spells: Magick of the Hanging Rope
The Goth Cathedral: Rituals of the Broken and Beautiful
The Cretaceous Codex: Dino Spirits and Fossil Magick
The Turkey Bones Ritual
Nine Lives of Manifestation: Unlocking Bastet's Reality Codes
Chaos Muscles: Building Strength from Twisted Pain
Emo Blood Magick: The Veins of Power
The 3AM Flood: Nighttime Urination, Sleep Loss, and the DI Spiral
The Silence Between the Stars
The Lemon Method: Sour Your Way to Success
Starlit Sovereign
The Rite of Twelve Gates: Walking the Gates of the Duat.
Cornbread and Conjure: Recipes for Riches and Rootwork
The Black Rose Rituals: Emo Love Spells and Obsession Magick
The Eternal Goodbye: Death Magick and Rebirth Rituals
Sinkrot: The Drain That Remembers
The Hybrid Mindset: Thinking Beyond Evolution
Bone Dry: Navigating Dehydration Before It Breaks You
Wreathcraft: Winter Sigils and Yuletide Spells
The Rite of Twelve Mouths

S'mores of the Damned: Haunted Recipes for Halloween Night

Rethink the Drink: A Beverage Survival Guide for DI Warriors

The Shadow Chord: Guitar Magick and Sonic

Malformed Yet Majestic: Leading When You Feel Wrong Inside

The Cursed Diary: Ink-Stained Spells of the Emo Soul

Anxiety Off Switch: Emergency Reset for a Fried Nervous System

The Energy Heist: How to Take Back Your Life from Drainers

Beyond the Bathroom: Rebuilding Your Social Life With DI

Coyote's Gift for Decision Makers

Ghoul-Goo: Spooky S'mores You'll Die For

Echoes in the Mirror: Scrying and Self-Destruction Magick

Thread and Thorn: Stitching Spells from Rural Cloth

The Mogwai Mind: Building Untouchable Wealth from Small Ideas

Be Your Own Guide: Trust Your Inner Compass

Hormones in Chaos: The Endocrine Puzzle of Diabetes Insipidus

ChronoCleanse: Detox Your Biological Timeline

The Limb You Hide Is the One That Saves You

Leaves, Bones, and Whisper Spells

The Dinosaur Mindset: Prehistoric Tactics for Modern Wealth

Clawing Back Control: A Bastet Method for Boundaries and Empowerment

Samhain Codes of the Forgotten

Orange Alchemy: The Autumnal Spellbook

Monster Within, Master Without

The Sigil That Sleeps

Hearthcraft: Yule Hearth Sigils and Winter Warmth Spells

Temple of the Purring Moon: Rituals from Bastet's Lineage
When the Earth Remembers Your Footsteps
Food for Mood: Eat to Heal Depression, Not Just Survive It
Witch of the Kudzu Vine: Southern Pagan Wealth Secrets
The Invisible Diagnosis: Advocating for Yourself With DI
The Coffin's Lullaby: Sleep Magick and Nightmares as Portals
Ashes of the Will: Rituals for Erasing the Self
The Fracture Rite: Shattering the Magickal Core
Funeral Candles: The Art of Emo Flame Magick
The Black Grimoire: A Blank Ritual for Writing in Absence
Phantom Thirst: A Halloween Survival Guide for Diabetes Insipidus
The Hollow Crown: Emo Royalty and Magick of the Outcast King
Sandpainting for the Soul
Falling Into Balance: Using the Extra Hour to Recalibrate Life
100 Southern Superstitions That Still Work
The DI Child: A Parent's Guide to Raising Hydrated, Happy Kids
The Jungle of Shame: Escaping the Hidden Lab of Doubt
The Witch's Toast: S'mores Spells and Creepy Confections
The Hoodoo Pantry: Spells from the Mason Jar
The Immortal Fortune: Secret Wealth Lessons from Captain Jack Harkness
The Specter's Embrace: Magick for Channeling Ghostly Lovers
Grateful Waters: A Thanksgiving Survival Guide for Diabetes Insipidus
The Seizure Gospel
Harvestbind: Autumn Sigils and Samhain Spells
Doctor Who: The Algorithmic Awakening
Silent Nights, Steady Waters: A Christmas Survival Guide for Diabetes Insipidus

The Extra Hour Effect: How One Hour Can Transform Everything

Blade Between the Breaths

Running with the Mountain Shadows

Echoes of the Failed Experiment – Becoming a Living Legacy

Swamp Witches & River Ghosts: Real Southern Hauntings

Cornbread Prophecies: Magical Recipes from a Southern Table

Doctor Who: The Signal in the Star

Bloomcraft: Spring Sigils and Equinox Enchantments

Vanisher: How to Disappear from the Internet Without Losing Your Life

The Ultimate Christmas Cookie Cookbook

The Unbreakable Parent: How to Mentally Survive Raising Kids in a Broken World

Time Debt: How to Reclaim the Hours You Didn't Know You Lost

One Month, One Million: Unconventional Cash Creation Tactics

Doctor Who: The Cyber Conversion Protocol

Black Friday Frenzy: The Art of Finding Hidden Online Deals

The Grimoire Buried Under the Apple Tree

Digital Couponing Masterclass: Your Step-by-Step Guide to Black Friday Savings

The Fire Inside the Flint

Shadows on the Ceiling: The Emo Guide to Astral Magick

The Bone-Eaters Beneath Us

Black Friday Bundle Blueprint: Creating Irresistible Product Packages for Maximum Sales

Thirteen Nights of Unbinding

Doctor Who: Engines of Influence

Pumpkin Spice Alchemy: Recipes of Fire and Frost

When Raptor Met Rexy: Prehistoric Lessons in Wild Romance
Oblivion's Candle: Burn the Path Behind You
Campfire Curses and Chocolate: A Halloween S'mores Grimoire
The Wallet That Wasn't Mine: Breaking Free from Inherited Scarcity
The Cola Zodiac: What Your Fizz Says About Your Fate
Frostfire Fortune: Unlocking Winter's Hidden Prosperity
Signal Jamming: Detox Your Brain from Info Overload
The Dust of the Forgotten Rite
The Golden Cat Sigils: Drawing Power in Bastet's Name
Mud Magick: The Prosperity of Getting Dirty
Savory Spicefall: Beyond the Pumpkin Pie
Pumpkin Spice Apothecary Kitchen
The Pumpkin Spice Economy: Turning Trends into Billions
The Ember Veil: 13 Nights of Fire Magick
Financial Freeze: When Earning Triggers Panic
The Gingerbread Alchemist: Sweet Recipes with a Twist
Biosynth Power: Programming Yourself from Scratch
Echoes from the Talking Circle
Truffle Alchemy: Fungus of Fortune
Spores of Power: The Truffle Witch's Handbook
Doctor Who: The Tower That Speaks
The Mycelium Veil: Truffle Magick Unbound
Broke But Ashamed: Healing the Shame Wound of Debt
The Evergreen Mind: Growth Through Winter Stillness
The Black Veil Truffle Rite
The Voice Beneath Symbols
Witchlight on the Bayou: Swamp Spells for Sovereignty
I Grew Up Poor and Now I Sabotage My Success
The Lantern of Hollow Souls

Shutdown Survival: A Citizen's Guide to Thriving When Government Stops

When Abundance Feels Like a Threat: Healing the Hidden Fears of Enough

The Scarecrow Grimoire

Owls of the October Veil

Candlewax and Curses: A Halloween Spellbook

Excavating the Inner Fossil – Transforming Fossilized Thoughtforms into Tools of Power

The Yule Witch's Spellbook: Magick for the Holiday Season

Haunted Christmas: Ghost Stories for Winter Nights

The Christmas Survival Guide: Thriving Through the Chaos

The Bone Orchard Rites

Haunted Commerce: The Ghost in the Marketplace

When Money Triggers the Inner Child

Silent Night with the Silence: A Christmas Thriller

The Lightning Crown: Living and Leading Through Seizures

TARDIS Tidings: Festive Stories from the Whoniverse

Autumn Reset: Slowing Down Without Falling Behind

The Trillion Dollar Soul: Rewriting the Currency of Reality

Truffle Eclipse Magick

Micro-Manifestations: Quick Magick That Works

5-Minute Rituals for Busy Witches

The Marshmallow Massacre: Halloween Treats with a Sinister Twist

Blood and Blackberry Thorns

Magickal Mornings: Rituals for a Blessed Christmas Day

Embers of the All-Hallows Fire

The Pumpkin Market Collapse

The Hour You Gained: Transforming Time Into Power

The Chamber Must Be Sealed: Mastering the Power of Controlled Access

The Cursed Manuscript of Petosiris

The Festive Hearth: Creating Holiday Traditions

Darkness Rising: Thriving as Nights Grow Longer

Harvesting Time: Turning the Year's End Into Your New Beginning

Petosiris and the 13th Zodiac Key

Wagewound: When Paychecks Become Identity Prisons

Walls That Watch

The Silent Feast: Rituals of Power in the Longest Night

The Distortus Legacy : Becoming a Deformed King in a Perfect World

The Hollow Masks

The Gratitude Furnace: Forging Gold from Thanks

Feast of Inner Gold: Eating for Energy and Enlightenment

Haunted Commerce: The Season of Spending Spirits

Fear Bonds: How Panic Creates Profit

Black Friday E-Commerce Playbook: Sales Tactics to Skyrocket Your Holiday Revenue

Budgeting for Black Friday: A Holiday Savings Planner

Haunting the Harvest Moon

The Warrior's Water: Emergency Preparedness for People With DI

The First Sip of the Year: A New Year's Survival Guide for Diabetes Insipidus

Doctor Who: The Thirteenth Node

The Unseen Struggle: Mental Health, Anxiety, and Chronic Thirst

The Hearth's Hidden Ledger: Counting Energies as Currency

The Gift Alchemist: Turning Any Offering Into Gold

The Papyrus of the Bound Spirit

The Magick of Leftovers: Transmutation in the Fridge

Frost and Fortune: Christmas Wealthcraft for the Modern Magus

Last-Minute Gifts: Creative Ideas on a Budget

10 Secrets to Surviving Holiday Crowds

The Witch's Dow Jones

The Witches' Graveyard Shift

Pumpkin Sigils: Carving Rites for Midnight Power

The Secret Shopper's Black Friday Guide: How to Get Early Access and VIP Deals

Fever in the Foundation

The Neuralyzer Reset: Reprogram Your Morning Routine

Lightning Lessons of the White Painted Woman

The Enchanted Snowflake

The Magic Sip: Surviving Disney Parks with Diabetes Insipidus

The One Who Draws Through You

Santa's Secrets: A Magical Holiday Planner

Silent Bells, Loud Miracles: Self-Help for the Season of Stillness

The Sugar Spell Codex: Confectionary Magick of Christmas

Autumn Hexcraft: Fallen Leaves, Fallen Barriers

Sleep Like a Fortress: Build a Life Where Insomnia Can't Survive

Nowhere Was Ever Home

Christmas Under the Stars: A Celestial Holiday Guide

Rentproof: How to Never Be Evicted Again

Workless: Escape the 9-5 Without Being Broke

The Gilded Gift: A Wealth Altar for Christmas Morning

The Black Friday Grimoire

The Hollowing: Ceremonies of Spiritual Collapse

Doctor Who: The Nameless Signal

Where the Eagle Hides His Courage

The Dwarf Tyrant's Ascent: Claiming Power in a World of Giants

The Currency of the Dead: Trading with Spectral Bankers

The Icebound Witch: Survival and Magick in the Cold

The Emergency Money Mind: Constant Crisis, Zero Calm

Thirst & Roses: A Valentine's Survival Guide for Diabetes Insipidus

Springing Into Clarity: Mastering the Energy Shift of Daylight Saving

Speed of the Nanotyrant: Agile Strategies for Life's Hunt

The 90-Day Reset: A Science-Backed Guide to Reinvent Yourself Before the New Year

The Coil of Thorns

Timegates Unleashed

Dopamine Fasting 2.0: Rewiring Your Brain in a World of Overstimulation

The Nanotyrannus Mutation: Embracing Your Differentiated Form

Unwritten January: How to Use the Blank Page of the Year to Re-Author Your Life

Feast of the Forgotten Spirits: Ancestor Magick for the Holidays

The Burnout Codex: A System for Thriving Beyond Stress

I Don't Deserve to Have Money

When the King Doesn't See You: The Shadow Predator's Guide

The Reset Ritual :A Guide to Shedding Last Year's Weight—Emotional and Physical—by Spring Cleaning Your Soul

Calendar Alchemy: Learn to Bend Time and Productivity around Your Natural Rhythms

The Mirror Contract: A One-Sentence Agreement with Yourself that Unlocks Real Change

The Nile Formula: Sacred Flow for Millionaire Minds

Forward Momentum: Productivity Rituals for the Lost Hour

Harvest Gold: Wealth Magick of Pumpkin Spice Commerce

The Magick of Christmas Lights: Illuminating Holiday Rituals

Cranberry Crown: Royal Self-Worth through Ritual Meals

Petosiris and the Worms of the Feathered Throne

The Evergreen Equation: Self-Help for Sustained Growth

The Rain Will Wash Us Away: Emo Weather Magick

Snowlight Shadows: Magick Under Frozen Stars

Doctor Who: Merger of Empires

The Light Within the Feast: Magickal Wealth of Yuletide Flame

Momentum Machines: Small Habits Designed to Snowball into Unstoppable Forward Motion

Calm Spells: Magickal Solutions for Anxiety Relief

Santa's Final List: The Naughty Never Leave

The Mystic's Guide to Banishing Worry

The Silence Dividend: Turning Quiet Mornings into Compounding Growth All Year

Charmed Stillness: Rituals to Ease the Mind

Blood Spiral Ascension

The Vanishing Heart Invocation

Crystal Calm: Harnessing Stones for Anxiety

The Nano Tyrant Code: Strength in the Small Predator

The Energy Ledger: Accounting Methods for Vitality, Not Just Money

Snowglobe Mindset: Shake Up Your Thoughts, Settle Into Peace

The Weight of the Feather: Anubis's Codes for Soul Balance

Pocket Peppermint Power: Tiny Rituals for Big Holiday Energy

Shadowkeeper of the Golden Jackal: Anubis's Path to Energetic Protection

The Witch's Breath: Anxiety Relief Through Magickal Breathing

The Tiny Ember: Pocket Motivation for Cold Days

The Twelfth Doctor: The Rebel with a Cause (Peter Capaldi, 2013–2017)

The Thirteenth Doctor: Breaking the Mold
(Jodie Whittaker, 2017–2022)

The Fourteenth Doctor: A New Beginning (David Tennant, 2022–2023)

The Fifteenth Doctor: Rewriting the Stars
(Ncuti Gatwa, 2023–2025)

Santa's Shortcut to Success: Micro Habits for a Better New Year

The Midnight Cocoa Manifesto: Comfort Rituals for Hard Nights

Why I Can't Save: Trauma Blocks to Financial Planning

Dino Brain, Mega Goals: Rewire Yourself for Savage Success.

Jurassic Profit: Unearth Your Inner Millionaire Fossil

Scales & Softness: Dating with Dino Heart

Carnotaurus Dreams.

Red Willow Thinking.

Reindeer Resilience: How to Keep Going When You're Exhausted

Candlewick Courage: Lighting Strength in Dark Seasons.

Elf-Mode Focus: Fast Attention Fixes for Busy Seasons

Futureproof Feelings: Emotional Skill-Building for Resilience No Matter What the New Year Brings

The 90-Day Rewire: Transform Your Neural Pathways Before Spring Blooms

Jolly Rich: Christmas Micro-Money Magick for Fast Prosperity.

Gingerbread Gratitude: Mini Practices for a Happier Holiday

Trauma-Spending: When Money Becomes a Drug

Goal Skeletons: Build Minimalist Frameworks for Resolutions That Last

The Snarl Strategy: Growling Back at a World That Silenced You

The Hourglass Reset: Reclaiming What the Clock Took

Yule Claw: Dino Rites of Light in the Darkness

Sacred Circles: Grounding Rituals for Anxious Souls

Clockstopper's Gut: Rebuilding the Core of Time

Winterfire Drive: Harness the Cold Season's Stillness to Ignite Deep Motivation

The 5-Minute Productivity Hack: Small Steps to Big Results

Light Ascending: A Self-Help Guide to Longer Days

Inner Economy: Trade Self-Doubt for Confidence Like a High-Value Currency

Simple Success: Decluttering Your Life for Better Results

The Resilient Mind: Thriving in Tough Times

The 2026 Playbook: Mastering the Year Ahead

The Spring Sleep Solution: Conquering Fatigue After Time Change.

The Hormonal Compass: Navigate Back to Your Youth

Golden Vision: Eating for Your Eye Color with the Power of Ghee

Lionhearted Love: Strength in Relationships

MiB Mindset: Think Like a Cosmic Agent

The Ladder of Small Wins: Climb Out of Stagnation by Stacking Micro-Victories

The Momentum Hour: Gaining More in Less Time.

The Year of You: A Self-Help Blueprint for Unapologetic Self-Ownership

The Dust That Watches You Back.

The Astral Parent

Shadow of the King: The Nanotyrannus Parable

Tiny Tidings of Triumph: Small Wins That Change Your Life

Dwarf Tyrant Rising: When You're the One They Overlook

Get Some Tarot cards: https://www.makeplayingcards.com/sell/apophis-occult-shop

Get some shirts: https://www.bonfire.com/store/apophis-shirt-emporium/

<u>Instagrams:</u>
@apophis_enterprises,
@apophisbookemporium,
@apophisscardshop
Twitter: @apophisenterpr1
Tiktok:@apophisenterprise
Youtube: @sg1fan23477
Hive: @sg1fan23477
CheeLee: @SG1fan23477

Podcast: Apophis Chat Zone: https://open.spotify.com/show/5zXbrCLEV2xzCp8ybrfHsk?si=fb4d4fdbdce44dec

Newsletter: https://apophiss-newsletter-27c897.beehiiv.com/

If you want to support me or see posts of other projects that I have come over to: **buymeacoffee.com/mpetchinskg**

I post there daily several times a day

Get your Dinowicca or Christmas themed digital products, especially Santa Raptor songs and other musics. Here: **https://sg1fan23477.gumroad.com**

Apophis Yuletide Digital has not only digital Christmas items, but it will have all things with Dinowicca as well as other Digital products.

www.ingramcontent.com/pod-product-compliance
Lightning Source LLC
LaVergne TN
LVHW022008200926
848481LV00007B/2287
* 9 7 9 8 2 9 5 4 8 0 8 9 8 *